CW01151189

THE SINGLE PARENT'S JOURNEY TO SELF-DISCOVERY AND RENEWAL

THE SINGLE PARENT'S JOURNEY TO SELF-DISCOVERY AND RENEWAL

AVERY NIGHTINGALE

Creative Quill Press

CONTENTS

1	Introduction	1
2	Understanding the Challenges of Single Parenthood	3
3	Embracing Self-Care and Personal Growth	8
4	Building a Support Network	13
5	Overcoming Guilt and Self-Doubt	18
6	Exploring New Opportunities and Goals	22
7	Finding Love and Creating a New Family Dynamic	26
8	Celebrating Self-Discovery and Renewal	30

Copyright © 2024 by Avery Nightingale

All rights reserved. No part of this book may be reproduced in any manner whatsoever without written permission except in the case of brief quotations embodied in critical articles and reviews.

First Printing, 2024

CHAPTER 1

Introduction

Family structures, although gradually, have evolved with the dawn of change in globalization and individuals have taken on careers that go beyond the already well-established spheres of employment at the expense of stability in families. As much as all inventions come to enhance human convenience, the challenge - to balance modern life in the grand scheme of things, is a familiar burden of realization quietly shared by many challenged by society in the surroundings of family networks today. The hardship and endless challenges center around a single effort pushing an individual undertaking in a physical engagement proven through pillars of society called families. So much is lost as a result is for society that author and motivational speaker Lisa Nichols confirms "as a single mother, I cannot afford to give into my circumstances". To seek constant growth and the best in fulfillment, the author went through self-discovery starting from the ground up with her child in hand. After her poignant journey, Lisa adds "if it impresses you, it does not impress me. I am transformed to it", and this submission became the founders of her new life's mission. Lisa's pursuit to sharing fulfillment soon pressured her into public speaking, as a way of inspiring individuals to grow to levels previously unseen.

It is never easy to lose a partner who is the father or mother of your children. In fact, a feeling of emptiness immediately replaces a sense of fullness that was always there. And later it dawns on one that the reality of managing an enterprise alone is life in its simplest complexity. On the pursuit to find meaning, individuals in this group (single parents) often take on gigantic roles and make enormous sacrifices often unseen or uncelebrated because they are ordinary and regrettably expected. It is confirmed because as the 'dead' partner mounts (yes that's often the word - I have not attempted chirping the fact) his/her last resting place, life is expected to go on.

CHAPTER 2

Understanding the Challenges of Single Parenthood

There is a significant struggle in single parenthood as we build a limit for what is considered delivery of the caretaking role, when all we have to do is to survive in those moments: to achieve self-sufficiency in the labor market after so long without dedicating our time specifically to our career; to discuss the truth about the divorcing process with our children; to set new objectives, new projects, as well as decide on the places to set down our roots. Many elements are in a state of constant transition in this phase; however, it may also be a time for increasingly liberating storage (construction of the single parent identity). At this point, when we continue to transform and rebuild the notion of "normal" of our family, it is extremely important to continue with an interest in the balance of the emotions of the children in the tone that emerges from all these changes.

As challenging as it may be to face the reality of being a single parent, understanding the journey of single parenthood, a concept I like to call the transition, can be very revealing. After divorce, we begin the initial transition (post-separation) with the normal thoughts of despair, or the feeling of having been unsuccessful in our attempt at reaching a lifelong goal. It is difficult to face the loneliness, changes, and adversities that come our way because the spouse on whom we were emotionally dependent (and to whom we dedicated our life and life projects) is not by our side any longer. Tumultuous thoughts may arise that range from feeling unworthy to those of hostility, or to a sense of relief in no longer wanting to maintain a relationship at whatever cost. We also may feel some optimism and high expectations because it ends up with a feeling of freedom and we are aware of the many opportunities that may come our way. The ambivalence luck remains within us.

2.1. Financial Struggles

Anna entered the empowerment forum at JP Morgan Chase and began to piece together her self-discovery and renewal journey. With guidance in financial empowerment and encouragement to let her artistry run loose again as Mother, her wonderful daughter, fondly calls her. "We as parents are the model, we are the orbit, they are our children - so what we do reflects on them," Anna expressed. "In the quiet storm of my harrowing state, I found myself in my stitches. Women have had a long tradition of adorning things and bringing beauty and color where possible. I decided to break free from my depression, with something vibrant. I made a call, whether a lunch bag to take to work or my favorite jeans spangled with colorful beads. I was no more impressed with the fancy lining of my overpriced bag or low-rise boot cut feature."

In times of counsel, it's not in the house of my friends I would rather walk to. I find comfort in art, design, and the sneakers I once loved so much. I got busy with making things - merely for the love of doing something I had control of. For a long time," Anna wrote in her personal blog. "I did not have what it took to act, nor the courage to be candid about the state I was in. One day it fell upon me a letter about JP Morgan's women empowerment forum and the life I lived, and regretted. I read that letter over five times and for the very first time, I allowed the hurricane to break the locks off the doors of my life."

When Anna Maria first became a single mother, the financial struggles were real and consuming. "Although I earned okay money, my expenses were high and things just somehow didn't stretch enough throughout the month," she recalled. "To make matters worse, I started comparison shopping, dining in the 2-discount restaurants with a coupon. It was mortifying and an all-time low for me in my life."

2.2. Emotional Rollercoaster

The emotional roller coaster ride that the single parent embarks on is one that can never truly be defined or come through in any way in which they might articulate the emotions. It is when the day-to-day responsibilities weigh heavily on their tolerance levels and grow towards becoming annoyances that parental responsibilities tend to become a not so amusing spectacle. Frustrations towards life and helplessness and self-pity tend to become an integral part of the career woman's emotions as she tries to grasp and come to terms with living the life of her slimmer, much diligent and younger, and perhaps more attractive self. And children too, as they become older, perceptive, and growing towards independence, often see a single helpless mom who has for too long been a successful career woman parent albeit dedicated physicians and district managers.

The way through single parenting is often laden with heartbreaks and unfulfilled expectations. Every event becomes magnified when viewed from the perspective of loneliness. This is further complicated if the child is residing abroad or in another locality for much under the full-time care and custody of the "better parent". Post divorce, parents are often forced to re-evaluate their priorities with single moms constantly juggling to balance their career and parenting role. Often the simple joy of daily learning of the unique little moments of shared lives become tainted with the shadow of a broken home and lives. It is a delicate balance of looking forward and yet sifting through remnants of a once-cherished past. There are times when things that went unspoken become mementos to a cherished past. The achievements of the child become tinged with sadness instead of anticipation that one has the backup and encompassing support of a significant other. These are harsh and yet bitter realities that need to be sifted through in every single parent's journey to establish individual growth, progress, and self-discovery.

2.3. Balancing Work and Family

We live in a society that has been bound by principles that have generally allotted the roles of parent and provider to each of a child's keepers. Mothers and fathers should, and have to be present in body and at whatever cost. They have to instill life virtues in their children in each and every single moment they can. To think any less is preposterous, and to turn a blind eye to the larger scope of things. Sharing responsibilities between custodial parents in today's world is impractical if both are to be able to keep pace with their daily work duties. Each of us is, like never before, in need of two-paycheck families to support the financially burning qualities of family life. This becomes an ever so tougher boxing match to win for the lone parent, whose hands are still full after the workforce has monopolized him/her. It is almost as impractical as a boat that has one paddle missing. Our financial support is inefficient, yet our families receive goods and services that are less so, just because we either don't have the time or the funds to see their procurement to task. Guidance has not been keeping pace with the dynamics of this generation's anxieties and letdowns; for children as well as parents! Deciding what is best for our families requires constant soul nurturing. To have familial profits grow, we have to selflessly perform the day-to-day that all too often leads the parent, alone, to corner themselves. Without time, financial solid support for the home will dwindle, and so too will the emotional resources that empower our families to reasonable and engaging living standards.

Certainly, with kids in the mix, life can get overwhelming for the single parent. As a single parent, I'm juggling more than I ever imagined. Amidst the never-ending pressures of family logistics, work and keeping it afloat financially, it's sometimes easy to believe that worry abounds. My priorities always lead back to my children, both emotionally and resourcefully. My work and finances are only the cycle for the life perspective I take. Finding balance for me is, at times, like trying to stand on the apex of a bike pedal. I tilt one way and work gets in the way of really getting a grip of the kids' needs; keep on going forward and the boredom of the day-to-day kicks in. The daily grind easily gets to me, as it leaves little space for benefiting them as best as I certainly have the ability to benefit them. On some detrimental days, the stress of the regular makes it all too easy for me to fall into the trap of believing stressful toil as being productive. All too often, I have caught myself in chains of life overwhelming strain. The beauty of it, though, is that by virtue of knowing we have to be somewhat pragmatic and having our little cubs to fend off for, we strive. The following post presents some of the balancing acts and strategies I absolutely swear by in trying to beat the mum and dad statistics of stress, getting over kidney failure, financial woes, and recent GQ lifestyle changes. They might contribute to a substantial easing of the regular pressures you might be encountering just now. I hope they provide you, hill climbers, with the insight they contain to keep our wheels rolling!

CHAPTER 3

Embracing Self-Care and Personal Growth

Parenthood alone can be lonely. My days are generally filled with social interactions at work but few day-to-day interactions other than with my kids. Over the years, being alone became my natural state. Whether it was my career or making plans to dine or vacation alone, it's what I had grown accustomed to. While travel or dining alone as a single person can be quite freeing and possibly empowering, routine isolation and boredom relating to having comparative field days (and dinners) with an imaginary person in your life seem like a modern-day tortured circle of hell. There is no destination or rest from pedantic sameness as you compare and contrast your previous experiences to your present boring regularities. Each comparison is a judge and jury highlighting the missing pieces of your existence.

My identity as a single parent for so long served as the crutch or excuse for not enjoying a fulfilling personal or romantic life. This is where you need time and the space created by self-care for self-improvement in increments of creativity, discovery, and growth. Boosted by daily self-care, you'll begin to work on who you are as an individual with an expanded mindset ready and open to new paradigms and opportunities in love, friendship, career, and in your overall personal life.

In allowing Q-time creativity and self-discovery, single parents slowly find their intrinsic joys in what seems like the absolute chaos of their lives. At first, I had no idea how important self-care was. I'd watch TV with my kids or channel my stress into making their lives fun and as normal as possible. But putting yourself last develops into an unrewarding pattern. If I took the time for myself to run a 5K or put myself together in a way that made me feel attractive, I developed the capacity to express love without a feeling of sacrificial martyrdom. The weariness of childrearing gradually lessened as I honored myself as an individual and began the process of self-discovery.

Daily self-care can seem both an aspiration and a burden for solo parents. Sleep, a prerequisite to reasonable emotional regulation, is often compromised by workload or by middle-of-the-night worries. Exercise and personal grooming—and anything that amounts to self-care—are often a lowest-priority luxury in the simplest of terms to increase what can often be already strained budgets. That said, to elevate from merely surviving to thriving, we must prioritize them.

3.1. Prioritizing Mental Health

The "how" of mental health really depends quite a bit on you as an individual. The most important tip I can share is the importance of connecting with people. So many of us end up isolated as single parents, and this not only fosters the feelings of solitude and loneliness currently gnawing at your mind but also keeps you out of reach of those that genuinely have your best interest at heart. Use social media to forge connections with parents and individuals lacking a romantic partner. Show up for yourself at public events and become a part of a community that resonates with who you are at the moment. Whether you feel you can only afford two or three hours at a time once per week, do it and do so regularly. This is what therapists mean when they advise you to build a positive support system around you. This brings me to my next important key to mental health: friendships. The loss of a lasting companionship (wife, husband) often leaves us without an anchor and a sense of kinship. Social media is a good tool for engagement as some people prove better communicators than others behind a screen. You won't form healthy ties without reaching out into the world and fostering a local group of friends, however.

The most important place to start with is our mental health. Single parents typically harbor feelings of guilt and resentment about their life situation, and when left unaddressed, these feelings fester and negatively affect every area of their lives. In extreme conditions, an individual can be rendered to such a state of mental anguish that mental illness ensues. For most of us, however, things do not reach great extremes before breaking. The great thing about being a single parent on a path to self-discovery is that we are capable of recognizing problems and addressing them entirely within. That's not to say that we don't require some help from family and loved ones when it comes to childcare. Neither does it discount the benefits of joining support groups and utilizing the last stitch of the safety net provided by government programs.

3.2. Establishing Healthy Boundaries

Before I focus on establishing healthy boundaries, I want to clarify the "authentically self". According to my coaching psychologist, who based her knowledge and understanding of self on Existential theory, the authentic self is innate and not only an understanding that one may have when challenged. The authentic self defines every action we take and every decision we make. It is the driving force for life and the cornerstone of our self-awareness, our relationship to ourselves, and our relationships to others.

Dr. Williams helped me to separate these four components of self through visualization and cognitive exercises. Together, these tools helped me find my direction, those deeply entrenched beliefs and emotions that directed me toward my maladaptive behavior. In my case, the journey to reclamation of self is long and fraught with difficulty. The journey, the story, and the challenge, however, differ for everyone, yet the first lesson in life revolved around establishing healthy boundaries. Now, while discussing boundaries, I will pencil in a footnote or two regarding authenticity.

During my first lesson from the coaching psychologist, Dr. Lisa Williams, we discussed the difference between my authentic self, my pseudo-self, my adaptively maladaptive self, and my maladaptive self. Every time she referred to the adaptively maladaptive self, I cried like a baby. In reality, my twin daughter and I are in excellent health, have a stable home, good childcare, and outstanding job security; in essence, everything is beautiful. Then why do I feel guilty when I take time for myself? Why do I feel like I am being selfish or hear my mother's ominous voice in the back of my head, chiding me about how "I think I'm better than everyone"? Initially, I could not answer this question, but eventually, I was able to pinpoint the source of the conflict within myself. My internal struggle was founded in the messages I received during my formative years. The guilt I felt was not born of reality but rather lived inside of me for years. The time for change had arrived.

So how do you effectively become your own source of support? Establishing healthy boundaries is a necessary first step. When setting boundaries (which reflect our beliefs, values, and attitudes), knowing who you are is crucial. Recognizing, accepting, and respecting the authenticity of self is a major component of self-awareness.

3.3. Pursuing Personal Interests and Hobbies

The artist that went on hiatus can be reborn. The breakdancer too can resume his old routine. Fears and self-doubt can also take a back seat during these pleasant activities. Delving into a world of a happy clam is the perfect antidote for the powerless single parent. It is also good criticism or concern. It is not giving up or abandoning everything. The label coward or selfish is just somebody else's opinion. Thus, one can relate to the different issues on a regular basis. Mutual support, the importance of friendship, joy in nurturing, and reliance with little financial rewards – all relevant and interesting. And the aspiring writer realized the experiences she considered ordinary are blog-worthy. By extension, her writing about unwanted dilemmas may eventually help somebody.

A little time for herself doing things she used to enjoy or new pursuits can make a world of difference to a single parent. Moms or dads too should not feel guilty. Even children deserve an independent and happy parent. Remember the safety instructions on planes after boarding? They advise putting the oxygen mask on yourself first before attending to your child. A struggling single parent may have mixed feelings about this, but now is the time to realize the importance of that precaution. Only a coherent and sane parent would be able to efficiently take care and make wise decisions for the children. Plus, children benefit from happy and fulfilled caregivers. Encouraging them to take part in activities promotes strong skills, confidence, and a sense of belonging. This should explain why one too deserves time away for personal rewards.

CHAPTER 4

Building a Support Network

There are many support programs that assist single parents emotionally, spiritually, financially, and practically. Local and national programs either provide information directly to single parents or maintain directories of programs and service organizations. It is important for single parents to become their own case manager and build a network of supporters. Healthcare professionals can answer many parenting questions and provide lists of agencies in the community that offer childcare and other practical services for parents. Most communities offer some type of training program that teaches parenting skills. It is important to assess your own skills and abilities before choosing a program. Some programs specifically teach Trust-Based Parenting, a style of discipline that many professionals believe is particularly effective for single parents. If the single parent prefers a traditional system of parenting, classes such as "Redirecting Children's Behavior" are offered in many towns. Classes focusing on self-nurturing skills like "Heart Right" and religious or spiritually-based programs like "Heart to Heart" are offered nationwide. It is important that the single parent's entire support network embrace their respective values and goals.

After a separation, single parents—especially young single parents—face these emotional, spiritual, practical, and financial needs mostly on their own. Furthermore, the social belief that marriage marks maturity and readiness for children contributes to a general perception that exists for some singles that they are not quite adults, even while they are thrust into the role of being fully responsible for another human being.

Every single parent has emotional, spiritual, practical, and financial needs that require attention. The traditional family provided many options to help fulfill these needs. A grandparent or stay-at-home parent could step into the primary caretaker's role for little or no cost. An at-home parent's attention supplemented the emotional needs of the growing child. Another parent acted as a role model for values and beliefs and provided love and affection to the primary caretaker that might not have been practiced within the family. In some cases, grandparents or other family members also saved education funds for their descendants. Additionally, nurturing relationships with neighbors and a generous extended family contributed to support.

4.1. Seeking Help from Family and Friends

When you are a single parent, you need to know that you are not alone. Sometimes when we go through a difficult situation, asking for help is actually our first step to become stronger. It's okay to ask for help, especially from people whom you love and whom you trust. It's far (far) from being a shame to ask for support - I could have sunk deeper into my grief if I never asked for it - it was probably the hardest part yet the most important. You can ask for a friend's help to remind you about your own strength, or simply by starting the day by recounting the kindness from the people around us. Ask for your closest family's help to take care of your kids when you have to do something or to financially help while you are still adjusting to the new situation. Yes, you are a single parent, but that doesn't mean that you have to do everything alone.

As we take care of our children, we think about our own future that seems so unsure and scary. We worry about our children's education and what is going to happen to our daily life in the future. It took me almost a month to ironically stop crying and start seeking help from my closest friends and family. I remember my best friend told me, "You can take a break in my apartment whenever you need." I asked my close friends for a bit of money to open a new spa, and I asked my dad to take care of the kids during the day because I had to work every day to support my family. My closest friends also helped me by spreading my CV around, and I got a new working opportunity that helped me to reprioritize my time for myself and my children.

4.2. Joining Single Parent Support Groups

With regard to the process of self-renewal, a single parent must therefore feel that his or her right to be adequate providers is proven in order to believe in oneself. The support that can be extended might not be monetary, but when the physical or emotional burden has been lifted, one should see the smile change on the faces of the children. The transformation in their character towards resilience develops an inner sense of joy. Despite personal failures, the single parent believes that the children are the single parents' gift to the world, as emphasized in the popular support groups. A person's joy after the encounter might be restored for the single parent who shared a truly non-material gift.

Single parent support is extended not only in the aspect of coping with the physical aspect of maintaining the family, but also in relating to the emotional aspects and tendency towards spiritual isolation of the children resulting from the effects of single parenthood in their lives. Single parent support also includes third parties who can impact the effects of single parenthood on the children in times when the single parent cannot help but be a single parent, either because of work or because of illness, states another.

Single parent support groups find the burden of single parenting more formidable by helping the single parent cope with the effect of single parenthood on all family members, breaking up the isolation that single parenthood fosters. Although located far away, single parents are given avenues to cope with each other through the connections created by single parent support groups. Single parent support groups become the venue for single parents who functionally feel that they are alone, or practically alone, with the weight of the world on their shoulders.

4.3. Utilizing Community Resources

Call me after you arrive from school. Notify other members when it may not be available. Most groups send reports about their activities, but the innate members show whether their intimacy is mature or late. Some members feel that the group 'assembly' is necessary, and young people have great respect. Attend all the family's important events. Since you are a group activity leader, encourage interaction between single parents, seek communication instead of 'activation', and instead choose quick and supportive discussion leaders. Make sure you are organized, web-efficient, and offer support, because if you are a religious education group, you can reserve space for parish carvers and other administrative functions that some members recommend zone. A group may have a more structured meeting each week, but there is no perfect strategy.

Community life (friendship) allows you to expand your emotional, informal sympathy and cooperation. Given the effects of self-assessment and interaction, cultural events combat personal horror, stress, avoid. Relax or quietly speak with 'friends' who can accept life as a single parent. Close friends reveal information about parenting compassion, friendship support, and self-confidence in their relationships and self and work meals each month.

Single parents may feel that they avoid listening to each other because they are less likely to be intimidated by the way parents see their partners, because parents feel less than them, or because the construction of eyes or community slavery is unstable and diverse. Community life has encouraged busy cooperation.

Try to end the day at your child's sports or extracurricular activity one day a week instead of coming here in the evening to the jamboree. Some small rural communities have clubs that meet in the middle of the week, local events, school activities, or libraries. Thus, he often visited the school or club that the child attended and began to know people who had the same responsibility or were married in similar ways.

Support groups for single parents, especially for mid-career parents, who need both the expressiveness and understanding of true feelings and freedom from the fear of 'talking about one's own personal emotional upset' that sometimes hinder conversation and hinder growth.

CHAPTER 5

Overcoming Guilt and Self-Doubt

You start worrying not only so they are happy, but to have they achieved to understand what you are feeling. They will think that they are quarreling because of them or, over time, feel the guilt of not having a perfect happy family. Under the same roof, whatever may happen, people always come up with more or less chaotic compromises. It's better to live far away and see your kids happy in a respectable environment, filled with love, joy, dedication, in a different way. Retrospectively, in the opposite case, they remain with unpleasant memories, mistakes, and frustrations at their own address, and finally, in the adult years, they respect you as a mother and worry for their children in an advanced manner.

It's easy to feel guilty and unsure of our actions as a single parent. After the separation, it's easy to be subjective. It's easy to blame the other parent, and sometimes it's even easier to hate the kids just to please the wrong side of the matter. Hold tight for all the strings you have in you now. Throw those negative feelings out of you. All this will just make everyone more unhappy. It fosters a hostile and stressful environment that slays all strengths and dreams. If the kids are too young, they won't understand what's going on, but they will certainly feel when all is not well. They absorb feelings coded in tears and too much silent conversation, while they yearn for laughter, unconditional love, attention, and physical contact.

5.1. Recognizing and Addressing Guilt

Recognizing and addressing this powerful emotion is crucial for the well-being of single mothers. Although guilt surfaces somewhere at the beginning of the process of renewing the self and discovering the new world, it can be overcome. Addressing the guilt requires courage, resilience, and developing a thick skin, for as women contemplate and find solutions in the inner processes, the environment around them is constantly pointing fingers and spreading rumors without really knowing the true nature of the dynamics of interrelationship. Very often, the woman is subjected to the opinions, attitudes, and behaviors of others. Even in people who are closest to her own family, friends, and most often, her own mother has difficulty in understanding and accepting new decisions and actions. It is not only about the essence and value but also about her own life choices with a potential ability to harm her own self-esteem. A single mother becomes the subject of social exclusion for being responsible for a socially onerous sin. She is blamed for her abandonment of tradition by deciding to leave the marriage and satisfy her inner needs.

Mothers who choose to be single parents often have to confront the specter of guilt. Society, directed by religious beliefs and many traditional moral teachings, tells us that single mothers have to be guilty because they dared to venture into the world of sin. Initially, the woman may experience disempowerment and hurt. The society plays an active role, subtly assisting with an agreement in her sense of devastation, discontent, distress, frustration, and sorrows. The single mother becomes the subject of social exclusion for being responsible and socially wrong doing. She is blamed for breaking tradition by deciding to leave the marriage and meet her inner needs. Guilt is a powerful tool for manipulation, and in this sense, it is very informative.

5.2. Developing Self-Compassion

How can we start being kinder to ourselves? Based on my experience, I must warn you that there will be resistance if you are following the steps accurately. We have been trained for years on doing and solving and productivity, and we may feel that we do not deserve to be loved, give ourselves permission to feel happiness, or respect our own worth because we recognized our limitations and perceived we need to reach standards we are trying to meet. One may still feel shame when promoting self-compassion, and because of that, he/she is the one who needs it. The first step of self-compassion is to recognize the suffering you are enduring and how much you long for relief. How should I feel? What do I have the right to be angry about? Would I be this harsh to a loved one? Once you become fully aware, you can move onto the second step.

This point follows naturally from the previous one, since research is demonstrating that self-compassion has beneficial psychological outcomes when dealing with personal failings and having a better relationship with other people. I wish that I had encountered self-compassion earlier on in my journey, either as a single parent or a unique parent, as this would have helped me deal with my negative reactions given all the changes. If there are only so many resources we can invest, I would bet on self-compassion alone to help improve your mental health and wellness. Can you spare just a few minutes per day to work on that relationship? You already invest a lot in other people, some of whom may not care. Who are you doing all of this for? Would you be more for the people who depend on you if you were kinder to yourself?

5.3. Celebrating Achievements and Successes

In my opinion, single parents need to accept and acknowledge their achievement and success. It's important to do so in a subtle way. Take a journey, visit an event, go for a picnic, or visit a place for lunch or dinner. An outing to the swimming pool, a water park, a telephone call to a distant relative after a success of your child, an ice cream we buy when coming back from a celebration, a visit to the museum after a success or a celebration of a sports game, are small but significant ways of celebrating success. Single parents don't stop their kids from having toys, dollies, tricycle, bike, ice cream, sweets, and so on, they also need some treat to make their strength perpetual in the long run. Successes and tiring moments are the major demographic phases that make the success more meaningful and eternal. We need to take some time and money occasionally out of the tiring journey we take, to greet and celebrate our success to keep the journey pleasant, successful, and motivating.

We need to recognize and celebrate our success and accomplishment. The Irish celebrated the saying "You take a drink when a child is born, when you get a promotion, and when you get a new job" and overwhelmed the everyday worries with an occasional celebratory drink that worked as a parent's ability to maintain self-confidence. Celebrating success is not just about having a drink, more significantly for a single parent, it is taking time to absorb and reflect on a success, to acknowledge, take time to realize and appreciate the magnitude of the success. The spiritual reflection that takes place when an individual is off the hook of day-to-day worries, issues, and when one is in a calm and happy mood. Day-to-day troubles, worries, constraints go away for the moment. Celebrating success prepares the single parents for the bigger responsibilities ahead. Successes add up like the small bricks used to build a house; they ultimately provide a meaningful castle to live in. I have caught one of my colleagues saying "I took my child out for an Italian dinner after she secured a scholarship." I felt that he was celebrating his daughter's success joyfully to internalize his success as a parent, and for his daughter to remember the day in her personal book of life.

CHAPTER 6

Exploring New Opportunities and Goals

Transitioning from being a married person to a single parent is a journey that creates a moment in your life's narrative that is the pivot point in your arch. Imagine yourself walking along one of those good walking trails that for some reason has steep ditches on either side. The slope into the ditches and the challenge of walking on the steep embankment creates the feeling of adventure. How well your journey goes depends on where you put your focus and what is eating at your energy and creativity. Intentionally engage in this journey that builds your strength and becomes one of your many accomplishments by adopting these principles and empowering precepts. Your ideals and principles will be your armor protecting you from the thieves of self-worth and decision paralysis.

There are many exciting possibilities awaiting you, but first it is important to recognize your limitations. Your new beginning as a single parent affords opportunities to shape the single-parent role you take and to mold the adult you are becoming. You can choose what to do with your time and energy, shaping your new identity and role. While your energy may be limited, your options are varied, and new dreams are waiting to be discovered as you grow into these roles navigating your new beginning creating a life of new opportunities and choices that all rest on you. There is no magical age at which your little darling is going to suddenly become perfectly capable of handling everything on his own. He is going to need you, at least in some capacity, for years to come.

6.1. Identifying Personal Passions and Dreams

Exercise a vision quest. Seek scientific and spiritual materials related to your sought-after changes. Speak more of your dreams. Speak about them to God, children, friends, other family, a trusted elder. Express your dreams to co-workers, employers, and your neighbors. Your dreams' description may bear an angel bearing a message for your actual truth. Be receptive. In particular, new mothers should believe in the rejuvenation of women's purpose. We are not bound for titled positions in an unsystematic rat race - chasing stardom; shadows along a receding horizon of material illusions. Let us recognize and believe in our calling as custodians, enlighteners, and peacemakers. Our work was not given to us as a punishment. Let's unlock our gentle, redemptive caresses within the stars, oceans, and skies. Our destiny is to lie fondly in the bosom of the universe.

This is how to rekindle our watered-down or snuffed out dreams:

Readers, you are not alone in this journey; do not despair. Our creator intends only greatness for us. Something beautiful happened to me as a single mother. I used to passionately long for scholastic success to aid my three boys' scholastic accomplishments. Although, it is commendable to sacrifice for children's scholastic progress; this was not the profile of my soul. So this particular year on the course to a doctorate in education, I became disheartened because my dreams as a child, to write creatively, were undergoing deep slumber. Then one day while researching my dissertation, I had a sudden epiphanic moment. I realized that I was in the midst of my change. I felt relieved that my identity was only hidden for a while. (Of course many mothers are able to strike a balance between their maternal and scholastic roles). Well this is when I uncovered my long-lost figure; my authentic dreams and my pleasing potential for global influence through words. I regained the natural courage to paint the world with a new, sweet aroma of sheer self-expression. To discover my divine potential was an effortless assignment. Nonetheless, to live up to my glowing potential, put my endurance and patience to the test.

6.2. Setting Realistic Goals

Another example of setting realistic goals is deciding you'd want to write a book. If you're a busy individual besieged with a multitude of other responsibilities, and who isn't an accomplished 'writer', does it really sound realistic to even assume you'll finish it at all? A goal to "begin work on a prototype of a book and finish four chapters" sounds far more realistic than something as definitive and heavy as "Write a book". This specific goal may even transform into something you once thought was absolutely unrealistic in the beginning.

What is a realistic goal? As a life coach, we set goals that excite and motivate our clients. At the same time, we remind our clients that they have to make sure that these goals need to be SMART goals where the acronym stands for Specific, Measurable, Achievable, Realistic, and Time-bound. Realistically, if you want to lose 50 pounds, it will be more realistic if you set 10 separate goals to reach that 50 lbs weight loss. One of those separate goals might be to join a gym, a diet, or to consult a dietitian. These are goals that are much more realistic than simply saying you want to lose 50 lbs all in one go. The goals need to be specific, measurable, and time-bound. If it was your goal to lose 50 lbs over the course of a year, then you need to determine when the 5 incremental weight losses will occur, how often you'll need to work out during those phases, how disciplined you need to be with food intake, etc. A short-term (or smaller) weight loss goal is so much more feasible to accomplish; hence making the overall goal very realistic.

6.3. Taking Steps towards Personal Fulfillment

The experience of motherhood, especially of the single mother, does not imply blocking herself with motherhood, because re-creating the human being is the constant point of her life. It is the total mother, whose own reinvention is the work of every day, in each family can, however, make her important life choices, because she has to pay for this with the flexibility result of an effort permanently sustained. Thus, Louro reinforces that women need to devote themselves to their own efforts and be tied to their aspirations in the multiple fundamentals of their condition of their existence as women who are mothers, daughters, lovers among other vital potentialities to carry out their project of personal and collective fullness.

Welwood writes that the parent who devotes all her time to the child, through an emotional attachment, often experiences an unconscious disappointment because the infant cannot react to the mother's need to be fulfilled as a person. This disappointment is due to the mother's exaggerated expectations of what her relationship with the child can provide. Therefore, he warns that the emotional imbalance experienced in this phase affects the mother's emotional stability and leads to an emotional dependence on the child, very difficult to correct later. On the other hand, Vantini and Oliveira record that the majority of the time, the mother reestablishes her own individuality and reuses certain references without losing nurturing consideration.

CHAPTER 7

Finding Love and Creating a New Family Dynamic

I am waiting for the love of my life to honor me with his time, his presence, his story. And after six years without love, I decided to escape from a relationship that was not meant for me and join other single parents in search of a special person. Only love does us part; the love for our children never fades. We will progress to the next phase of our relationship, and I will continue to honor the person who is the father of my children, their creator, their protector; perhaps one day their friend. Our home is a safe place, and I am working very hard to make our dream a reality. My single parent life has been most joy-filled. My Divine right awaits.

Six years as a single parent pass in the blink of an eye, and within those six years, my children are transformed from babies to great little people. They are offering me the world and piling so much love into our home. We have grown together in such completeness that life makes sense, and hope, as always, precedes us. And in my moments of a higher level of consciousness, I too could not fathom living within any other reality. I am at complete peace. I am a single mother. I put an immense song in my heart, and I remind them often as to why being wrapped in my arms is the best place in the world. That is what I promise to give them through my love.

THE SINGLE PARENT'S JOURNEY TO SELF-DISCOVERY AND RENEWAL

7.1. Dating as a Single Parent

No person will be completely specific to you. If you have children, be aware that some children are pretty darn close at times. Women who are single will behave as if they will not date men without giving them a clear understanding. Some of you will weigh on the effects or are after getting in the way to make sure that their dream single men will continue on as a casual parent. In many cases, men do not want to date single mothers. Quite a few unmarried women eventually become single mommies. These women have undergone cruel experiences. This happens if you take the time to meet the wrong man. You used to be able to catch this man. You may not have enough qualifications to make the only man's interest. If you feel you do not, confidently, you will be left wondering where to go about finding the right person. When he finally leaves, your attitude will be weak. In fact, the knack of your private room will push you to drill. Your mental disability will realize that your chance in life is still given, which it does not. Your heart is determined that you are left remaining in society at the heart of the family-disliking club.

As a single parent searching for a significant relationship or a marriage partner, we all know that it is going to be a real challenge. Most of the issues we will encounter with dating are specific to us. However, there are issues which are more challenging if we are raising children alone. My initial attempts at dating were fast. However, as a single mother, it seemed to be difficult as no one wanted to date me. If they accepted, most of the men are pushy, hurtful, and terrifying. In order to avoid these situations, I made the decision to delay my relationship and stay single for a while. As a result, I made some apparent self-discovery. One of them is what I present to you – giving the advantage of the question.

7.2. Introducing a New Partner to Children

Respecting their pace is very important. We are taking it one day at a time, as pathetically cliché as that sounds. It is quite challenging for my daughters, given that I am super mom in all its functioning glory. I am still struggling with spending time with them and with communicating properly with my Mr. Best. There were a few snags as well. The only reason why we are managing is because I have clear set priorities; everything else just has to come second to my daughters because, like what my girls wrote in their letters to me, "We belong to you." Set routines are also helping out a lot. Now, we have our Monday, Thursday, and Sunday affair, though it can be quite challenging for weekends since most of Mr. Best's events occur on weekends and weekday evenings.

The day will come when we meet someone who matters to us, and we would want that someone to meet our children. He or she will meet the fruits of the most important chapter of our lives: our children. This signifies that we are already secure enough with our decision to involve the person in our lives. But then, it will not necessarily be a comfortable moment for the kids. They have grown used to having you all to themselves, and the addition of a new figure may not be easy for them to accept. In turn, there will be a lot of juggling to do. Real life is not the stuff that reality shows are made of.

7.3. Blending Families and Creating a Supportive Environment

Mothers who have lost love through abandonment, economic hardship, a return to the family home, people placing unwarranted blame on them for their difficulties, and even infidelity on the part of the fathers of their children need to rebuild their lives. The community loves to excommunicate women! Single mothers face adversity, and the legacy of hurt can last a lifetime. The love that we are made of is detached and only partially ours. We need tools and support to rebuild ourselves, and understand the environment we work within.

I have been blessed with eight step-children. We are a blended family and welcome the opportunity to love and share our lives with one another. Not everyone is this lucky! Not all blended families work the same way, as each person has his or her own history and set of difficulties that they bring with them. Under the right circumstances, family structures will be supportive. When synergy is present, the blended family can easily adapt to the introduction of different members. This can form the basis for everything both parents and children need for growth and development, because love, support, respect, and understanding are abundant. The past is not important, stability is. However, the environment created must be planned and agreed upon by all. Each person brings many things to their new family, so the base created must be one of growth and trust. Openness and communication are what will help nurture these treasures. Each person must listen that's in love! Love is present when we want others to understand themselves, and to express themselves… Let go of our love for them, but remain near!

CHAPTER 8

Celebrating Self-Discovery and Renewal

I have observed people. I have sought out knowledge. I have assessed situations. I have logically tried to make the right decisions. I have taught myself to think like those who have gone through similar or worse situations, and emerged from them in one solid piece. When the results are positive, it is one internal applause. Of late, I have not been lying to myself that any cute dress will make me change into Oprah. I know it may not be reasonable. For me to reach a fraction of her status, I have to think bigger and get comfortable doing things that women like her do... make decisions, thus controlling my life... my destiny. Knowing who I am has and continues to teach me to respect myself. Since I command respect for myself, others also respect me. It is a great feeling combined with the consciousness that my successes or failures, likes and dislikes are mine. I own them alone.

Any single parent going through the valley of despair, despondency, may doubt if this joy is possible. I know it is not an overnight thing. I did not achieve this state of mind overnight. It has been a long, lonesome journey riddled with hope, yes, but doubt and fear as well. There have been moments of extreme stress accompanied by high blood pressure whose closest cause was problems with money. It has felt a steep climb to self-discovery and consciousness, but it was always one deliberate step after the other. At some point during this journey, I realized fear was there to make me run quicker and jump further. Now I handle it calmly and carefully analyze its warnings.

Today I live in peace with myself. It is a great place to be. I have discovered who I am truly inside without the mask. The journey has included a lot of self-forgiveness, self-acceptance, the acquisition of knowledge, development of my talents, identification of and proper use of the potentials and abilities I possess, and effective management of the relationships I maintain or establish. I have also learnt not to overly depend on others for my survival to avoid unnecessary heartaches and disappointments.

8.1. Reflecting on Personal Growth

For long, I couldn't notice the growth within me. After all, don't we all grow? However, as time moves on and situations change, I can appreciate how much Freda has grown emotionally and intellectually. Growing as a single-pronged parent, someone once described me in that manner. I was offended long ago when someone defined me as a single-pronged parent. Now, I understand the dictionary meaning of the word, and that is exactly who I am. I am a parent who is alone or who has to do all the chores alone. Unlike when a person has two truly reliable hands who are 24/7 ready to lighten the caregiver's responsibilities, I have only one. The unfolding journey brought me to my strengths and weaknesses. I savored my success and loss. These experiences, both bitter and sweet, have shaped a unique, strong, and carbon copy personality of the person my children know as their only living parent.

From time to time, it is important to reflect on the changes that occur in us as individuals. We often take for granted the growing process since it takes time for the changes to be prominent in our lives. A few years when we are faced with a new challenge, we look for answers and solace, and more often than not, we feel the gaps within us. Change is uncomfortable, and so we tend to resist because we feel the need to reflect on our life, and often this makes us question our beliefs. This is what I have seen in my friends and families over the years. When I look back on myself thirteen years ago, I do not see a young woman who was strong enough to be where I am now. Instead, I see a woman who was naive, emotionally weak, seeking love and assistance from friends. I was a woman who reflected on the loyalty and love bestowed upon me by my friends and their families. I was dependent on their judgment, on their wisdom, on their comfort. A woman in pain of being abandoned by the people I had trusted so much, and a mother who was swept off her feet in one blow, feeling the loneliness and the burden of responsibility to two precious lives. She was the woman who feared the future of her two young children.

8.2. Embracing a Positive Mindset

For a long while, mom thought of herself as finding her days to resonate with these words. My husband having self-removed himself from the lives of his ever-not-smiling-enough family was devastating to our family of 5, his absence being felt for years by those of us who didn't make the fateful choice of abandonment. When he left, mom was left with three school-aged children to raise on her own. The oldest was nine, the youngest had just turned three. It was after having our baby girl that we would learn the rosy path of 50-50 parenting would give way to one of legal battles for my own parental rights. We found us running around her newborn days like they were chaos-filled days where we felt nothing more than scalded by flames. We would lose them. Our childhoods. Our happiness. Mom found herself swimming through many moments in those early elephant grey days to keep her head above water.

My mom had operated in survival mode for so long that she had all but given up on the possibilities of her future. Parents everywhere would do well to remember that who we were – and what we were capable of – didn't end when we became mothers. We need only to recall the tenacious mother love exhibited by our animal counterparts in the wild to remind ourselves the lengths human mothers would go - the depths we would suffer - for our own beloved children. Just the single-minded pursuit of whatever is necessary in order to provide for our child?

Instinctive and natural. Where I found difficulty was in believing the future held possibility beyond making sure I'd be a better-than-greatest mother to my group of treasures.

8.3. Inspiring Others on a Similar Journey

A mentor coming from a place of enlightenment and shining illumination, exuding love and truth, has need of nothing more than the wings of the morning, his whispers, and heart of heavenly joy. He has successfully trained others to teach themselves, and they invariably come to him when a genuine issue of guidance arises. He is no longer on the single parent path—though he watches its twists and turns with an amused detachment—but guiding others on and off it, depending on the past life trajectory each person has drawn as their life's blueprint. Perhaps in another life, he too will help them achieve such mastery.

Yet, enthusiasm isn't just stationary (or it shouldn't be). So it follows, helping others on their journey adds a fresh helping of inspiration to the single parent's energies. Inspiration leads to more experience, experience synthesizing into wisdom, wisdom into enlightenment. Then —oh, so gently—the single parent becomes a true mentor. Such a one is able to direct others without them being aware of it, skillfully easing problematic situations and soothing spirits in distress without having to wrack his. Being of service has become so instinctual to him it's no longer calculated.

If the single parent has mastered most or all of the stages of the path, he is gifted with a new energy called enthusiasm. One reason enthusiasm is so called is because it's infused with the breath of God. Spiritual life, love, and truth have become one. With the thrill of new knowledge in his heart, the single parent feels called to inspire others on a similar journey. Coming from a space of competence, he offers: "I've been there, I've done that; come, and let me be a guide—for enlightenment, after all, is no solo bird. Birds of a feather flock together."

Milton Keynes UK
Ingram Content Group UK Ltd.
UKHW040939081224
452111UK00011B/234